W9-BLV-718

What he really did
and why it really matters

What people are saying about Original Jesus

Brilliant. Quick, easy, and to the point, Original Jesus unmasks the frauds and presents the real thing.

Dr Josh Moody, Senior Pastor, College Church, Wheaton, IL

Like a friend, this book helps sort through the question of who Jesus is. It points to the original Jesus in a lively and conversational way, so that we interact with voices all around but hear finally the words of Jesus himself. This book is like the best kind of friend, bringing us to meet Jesus.

Kathleen Nielson, author and speaker;
Director of Women's Initiatives at The Gospel Coalition

Carl provides a succinct and sincere presentation of the gospel for those willing to challenge their own presuppositions about Jesus. Here is a reliable guide to discovering that the Original Jesus is far more powerful, far more radical, and far more gracious than we have ever allowed him to be.

Dr Stephen T. Um, Senior Minister, Citylife Presbyterian Church, Boston;
President, Center for Gospel Culture; Author, Why Cities Matter

Excellent. Carl's lively and engaging style makes the gospel of Jesus, and everyone's need for him, explicitly clear. This is a great introduction to the true Jesus.

Gavin Peacock, former UK soccer Premier League player with Chelsea;
Missions Pastor at Calvary Grace Church, Calvary, Canada

Our culture loves to reinvent Jesus in its own image. This tremendous book gives us a strong and thrilling dose of reality.

Jared Wilson, pastor and blogger; author of Your Jesus is Too Safe

This is a book worth anyone's time. Carl simply and attractively walks through the Gospel of Luke and speaks into our culture in a simple, interesting and relevant way. I loved reading it, and I'd love my friends to read it.

Rico Tice, Founder of Christianity Explored Ministries;
co-author of One Life: What's It All About?

The real Jesus is more compelling, unpredictable, and life-changing than the image of him we tend to have in our heads. This engaging, witty and punchy book shows why.

Sam Allberry, pastor; author of Lifted and Connected

Contents

Introduction

I can still feel the crushing disappointment. I was eight years old, sitting in my classroom, drawing a truck. This involved looking at the model truck on the table, and drawing what I saw. It seemed so simple.

But as I looked at my efforts, I realized it wasn't simple at all. What was on my paper looked nothing like what was on the table.

There were two options for why it had gone wrong. Either it was my fault; or it was, somehow, the truck's fault.

I blamed the truck.

I got a new bit of paper, and started to draw my mom. I'd seen her every day of my life. How hard could it be?

Ten minutes later, I surveyed my masterpiece. Mom looked worryingly like a bad drawing of a truck.

On the plus side, it was better than my brother could do—though he was much younger than me, and was still drawing our parents with their arms coming out of their heads. And I did have some bits right. My mom has a head in real life, and she did in my drawing (even if it looked like a truck wheel). And she has four limbs, and so did my drawing (though one of her legs also resembled a truck wheel).

I had to face the reality. I was rubbish at art.

The real thing

In the end, there was only one positive point from the whole experience. I didn't really need a picture of my mom—because I had the real thing. And no drawing, even if Marie Childs (the art queen of my class) had drawn it, could capture who my mom was; could display her love or care or generosity, her smile or laugh or frown.

No sketch, however good, can tell you everything about a person. It can never fully capture the original. That's why we don't marry a portrait or make friends with a photo. We don't treat people as though they can be summed up by a quick sketch.

Except Jesus.

The general thinking is that we should view Jesus as an image—not on paper, but in our minds. Most of us have taken at least a quick glance at Jesus at some point in our lives—perhaps from going to church, or as our parents talked about him, or from a book we once read—and we've got a rough mental sketch of him. Perhaps your sketch has been built up carefully over the years; or maybe it was drawn years ago, and you haven't looked at Jesus since. Perhaps your view of him is as a good teacher; or a religious rule-keeper; or a story for children. Whatever works best for you.

That's how I viewed Jesus for years. I had an image of Jesus that worked for me. When he stopped being what I wanted, I re-drew him into a different Jesus, to fit in with how I wanted to live. It was easy and it worked.

But then I found the Original.

Meeting the Original

It turned out that Original Jesus—the one who lived in human history, who walked, talked, ate, slept, cried—was far better than any image I'd been offered, even in church. He was more interesting, more controversial, more unpredictable, more relevant, more, well, real.

And that meant that, in mistaking my mental sketch for the real thing, I'd been missing out.

So this book is about Original Jesus. He may well be very different to the "Jesus" you thought you knew, or who you've left behind at some stage. But he's real.

In each chapter, we'll look at a popular image of Jesus, and see how the original compares. And each chapter is in two main parts. First, **▶ What he really did**—what Jesus actually said and did. In each of these sections, you'll see some words in **this kind of text**. These are words taken straight out of the Bible* and are the really important ones. Those in normal text are written by me, just to help you grasp what was going on.

And then second, in **▶ Why he really matters**, we'll see what difference the things Jesus said and did 2,000 years ago make for our lives, hopes and futures today.

Let's meet Jesus—the Original.

---

* I use sentences from the Bible to show what really happened in human history. If you want to know why, you might like to flick to "Yes, but... isn't this all made up?" at the end of the book on page 55.

1.  Good teacher

Who was your favorite teacher? I don't mean the one you liked because you could get away with anything. I mean the one who helped you by explaining things in a way which meant that the completely confusing became crystal clear.

Mrs Mayner, my geography teacher when I was 13, was someone who helped me understand the world around me. For instance, she explained rain—why it falls, where it falls, when it falls. And sometimes she would predict rain—she had an amazing ability to look outside at 9.30am and correctly forecast that it would be wet at lunch.

But what Mrs Mayner couldn't do was control the rain. That's more than any geography teacher, anywhere at any time, has ever been able to do. Explain, yes. Predict, possibly. Control, never.

So Mrs Mayner was great in the classroom. In a storm, though, there wouldn't be much she could do. And in a sinking boat in a storm, there's not much anyone can do…

▶ What he really did

By the time he was thirty, Jesus of Nazareth, an ex-carpenter from a backwater town in northern Israel, was getting a reputation. He traveled from town to town, teaching and healing. He talked about God, about heaven, about life and death. Everyone came to hear his teaching. He had become a local celebrity.

Everywhere Jesus went, twelve of his closest friends—his disciples—went, too. Some of them had been fishermen, and there was also an ex-tax collector, a guerrilla fighter and a thief.

One day Jesus said to his disciples, "Let us go over to the other side of the lake." So they got into a boat and set out* across Lake Galilee, an inland sea about eight miles wide. Four of the disciples knew the waters well; they'd fished there for years. They could cross with their eyes closed—unless there was a storm.

As they sailed, Jesus fell asleep. A squall came down on the lake, so that the boat was being swamped, and they were in great danger.

The disciples went and woke him, saying, "Master, Master, we're going to drown!"

He got up and rebuked the wind and the raging waters; the storm subsided, and all was calm. What had been mountains of waves was now a millpond. "Where is your faith?" Jesus asked his disciples.

A wave of relief swept over the boat. But it was followed by fear and amazement. The disciples asked one another, "Who is this? He commands even the winds and the water, and they obey him."

READ THE FULL STORY Luke chapter 8 verses 22-25

▶ Why he really matters

Jesus was such a good teacher that men and women were willing to leave their jobs behind to travel around with him. He was such a good teacher that, 2,000 years later and throughout the world, people still remember that he said: "Do to others what you would have them do to you" and: "Do not judge" and: "A tree is recognized by its fruit." His wisdom is the most quoted in human history.

* Words straight from the Bible are in this kind of text.

But just for a moment, imagine if a good teacher—a man who could explain and sometimes even predict your life—was *all* Jesus was. If that image summed him up completely, by the end of that storm he would have been a drowned good teacher.

If the most interesting thing about Jesus was that he was a good teacher, there would have been twelve funerals around northern Israel the next week, as various mothers said: "I told him not to give up on the fishing/taxing/fighting/thieving. I told him not to follow that teacher, but he wouldn't listen."

And as they fought the waves swamping their boat, the disciples were expecting to attend their own funerals very soon. Several of them were experienced fishermen. You didn't fish if you were soft or got seasick. These were hard guys. But even they were panicking, because they knew they were sinking. All they had on their boat was a teacher—and a teacher is useless in a storm. They were going to die.

Undrowned

And then Original Jesus did something that no teacher throughout history has ever done.

He controlled the weather. Effortlessly and instantly. With just a few words.

Then he coolly, calmly turned to his friends as they sat, drenched, distraught, but amazingly undrowned, and said: "Where is your faith?"—"Why didn't you trust me to sort it out?"

Those twelve men got onto a boat with a teacher. They got off it with a man who was more than a teacher. They got off asking: "Who is this man?"

A simple answer

Actually, they should have known the answer to their own question. Both the Old Testament of the Bible (the bit written before these guys were born), and common sense, state that the answer to:

"Who can control the weather with a word?" is: "The one who made the weather with a word."

There's only one category big enough for a man who can tell wind to shut up, and order waves to behave. God.

That's why the disciples were trembling at the end of their trip. They were beginning to realize that Jesus was, and is, a good teacher who explains life and predicts life—but that he's so much more than that. He's the one who made life; the one who controls life.

Here is God who is a man. A real man, who sleeps, has friends, walks and talks. Yet a real man who is really God.

The end of guessing

This is very exciting. Our own ideas about God have to be based on guesswork. It's like me sitting down and trying to draw a picture of your mother—I might get her hair, her skin color, height and so on right, or I might get them totally wrong. But either way, I can't know, because I've never seen her.

So it is with our best efforts to work out who God might be— whether he's there, what he's like, what he thinks of us. We can only ever guess…

… unless he shows us.

And, on that boat, that's exactly what he did. God had come to earth as a man, to show us who he is. To prove he exists. To let us know what he's like. We can look at Jesus, and see God.

I don't know how you imagine God, if you do at all. Maybe a powerful, distant being who has far better things to do than think about you or me. Maybe as a nice old man in the sky with a beard. Maybe a tyrant who hates fun.

Well, here's the real God. He's a surprising God. A God who gets involved. Who has power. Who helps people.

A God who became a man and stood on a boat in a storm and said: "STOP," and was instantly obeyed.

The guessing about him can stop. God has stood in this world and said: "Here I am."

The best teacher

If you've always thought of Jesus as a good teacher, you're absolutely right. He's the best teacher there is, on every subject there is. His words are not just good teaching, they're God teaching. He's more than a lifestyle coach—he's the life creator. Because he made everything, knows everything, and directs everything, his teaching is always true, and his advice is always right.

Jesus is a good teacher... a great teacher... and he's so much more, too. What he did on that boat makes him more interesting, more exciting, and worth taking more seriously than any other teacher. In Jesus, we meet God.

Next time you're caught in the rain, Mrs Mayner could explain the water cycle to you. She might even have warned you to take an umbrella. But she isn't controlling it.

Jesus is.

That's what the disciples were beginning to realize. The fear of the storm lay behind them. But the most terrifying part of the day still lay ahead...

2.  Distant God

How are you with horror movies? There are two responses to properly scary ones. You might be unaffected by them—they're funny, and they're fiction, and you watch them and then go do something else. Or you might be terrified by them—you watch them, and then you can't sleep.

I'm firmly in the terrified group. Now that I'm old enough not to feel the need to pretend I'm cool, I just don't watch them. But for years, when a housemate or friend put a horror film on, I would sit through the whole thing with my eyes shut. *Blair Witch Project, The Exorcist, The Omen*; I've seen the opening and closing credits of all of them.

Why? Because, basically, I'm soft. When the going gets hard in any way, I tend to run away. And so, if I'd been in the boat with Jesus as it reached the beach… if I'd seen what Jesus saw as he stepped onto land… I'd have been back in the boat, rowing hard for the opposite shore, before you could say: "Chicken!"

▶ What he really did

Jesus and his undrowned disciples **sailed to the region of the Gerasenes, which is across the lake from Galilee,** Jesus' home patch.

When Jesus stepped ashore, he was met by a demon-possessed man from the town. For a long time this man

had not worn clothes or lived in a house. Instead, he lived in the tombs.

When he saw Jesus, he cried out and fell at his feet, the demon making him shout at the top of his voice, "What do you want with me, Jesus, Son of the Most High God? I beg you, don't torture me!" The impure spirit was terrified because Jesus had commanded it to come out of the man.

This evil force had made this man's life a misery. Many times it had seized him, and though he was chained hand and foot and kept under guard, he had broken his chains and had been driven by the demon into solitary places.

Jesus asked him, "What is your name?"

"Legion," he replied, using the word for a battle-group of 5,000 men, because in fact many demons had gone into him, not just one.

A large herd of pigs was feeding there on the hillside. The demons begged Jesus to let them go into the pigs, instead of into the "Abyss" of pain and destruction, and he gave them permission. When the demons came out of the man, they went into the pigs, and the herd rushed down the steep bank into the lake and was drowned.

When those looking after the pigs saw what had happened, they ran off and reported what Jesus had done. The locals came and found the man from whom the demons had gone out, sitting at Jesus' feet, dressed and in his right mind.

And they were afraid.

All the people asked Jesus to leave them, because they were overcome with fear. So he got into the boat and left.

READ THE FULL STORY Luke 8 v 26-39

▶ Why he really matters

Distant Jesus is a god who keeps his distance. He's out there, somewhere, and he politely never intrudes by coming too close. He lets us get on with our own lives. He never makes any demands... or makes any difference.

If Distant Jesus had walked up that beach, and suddenly he'd seen, running towards him down the path, a man who was clearly completely deranged, screaming at the top of his voice... he'd have done what I would do. He'd be back in the boat, steering clear, staying away.

Distant Jesus is nowhere to be seen when evil is about. And in our world, as on that beach, evil *is* about. You don't have to live long to realize that, while there is a lot that is beautiful about the earth, and about people, there is also a lot that is horrible. Happiness is only temporary, and partial.

Every day, we experience impulses inside us and influences around us that drag us down. And the Bible says that there's a spiritual person who stands behind those impulses and influences. He's called the devil, and his foot soldiers are demons. They hate God, they hate good, they hate joy. They are opposed to human happiness.

What to do with evil

All of us will have responded to that previous paragraph in one of two ways; because there are only two things we can do with the idea of the devil and evil.

One is to deny it's real. We live as though what you see is all you get. There's nothing "out there," so there's no devil. It's fiction. This makes it hard to explain where evil comes from, but most of the time we can ignore it anyway (particularly while it's only affecting other people). We would walk up the beach, see the guy coming towards us, hear him say that he's demon-possessed... and walk past, because there are no demons.

And if I were the devil, I'd be really pleased if everyone denied my existence; it would leave me to get on in peace with my work of opposing God, resisting good and destroying joy. As one of the characters in *The Usual Suspects* (another film I watched most of with my eyes shut) says: "The greatest trick the devil ever pulled was convincing the world he didn't exist."

But the only alternative to denial is terror—and no-one wants to live in terror. If you know there's evil, and that it's more powerful than you, you live in fear of it. It dominates you.

Enter Jesus

Denial and terror. Those are the two responses to the reality of evil.

Until Original Jesus walks up.

He doesn't stay at a distance. He doesn't need to deny the existence of evil, or to be terrified by it. When confronted with a whole army of demons, who would like nothing better than to cripple or kill this God-man, Jesus doesn't flinch. He walks up to the guy; he gives the demons an order; and he sends them into some pigs so that everyone can see what evil does—ruins, wrecks, destroys.

When it comes to opposing something that is wrong in the world, Jesus opposes it. When it comes to standing up to something that has gone wrong in a person, Jesus stands up to it.

It's awesome, when you think about it. These demons had completely controlled a man—even his speech. They'd even changed his name to Legion. No one had been able to do anything, even armed with chains. But with only his words for weapons, Jesus confronts evil, and triumphs over and destroys it. The guy who began alone, broken and crazy, heading for the same fate as those pigs, ends up "sitting at Jesus' feet, dressed and in his right mind."

Distant Jesus isn't there for us when we need help. He isn't there when evil of some kind is winning. When we cry out to him (and most of us do, at some point), he's nowhere. Original Jesus can help, does help, and will help.

That's what that guy discovered. That's what all the people who saw what had happened realized…

… and then they asked Jesus to go away.

Leave us alone

It's remarkable. "All the people asked Jesus to leave them, because they were overcome with fear." They see his power, they see he can help, and they say: "Please leave us alone."

Why? Perhaps because they'd rather live in denial, even with evil in their midst, than accept that Jesus is the real God, who won't stay at arm's length so that life can continue in the way that's most convenient or comfortable for them. They seem afraid of what might have to change if they let God get involved in their lives.

Distant Jesus is an easy "god" to live with. He's happy for us to believe in him but never to know him, or speak to him, or listen to him. Distant Jesus doesn't make a difference to anything—doesn't mind what we do, or how we use our lives, or how we pursue what we want in life.

Original Jesus, on the other hand, isn't an easy God to have. He'll come close, he'll get involved, he'll change things. He won't stay distant—but he will make a difference.

So it's easier to do what the people of Gerasenes did—ask Original Jesus to leave rather than invite him to stay. But it's better to do what the man formerly known as Legion did—stay as close to Jesus as possible. Because, when things get hard, when things go wrong in us or around us, Original Jesus can help, and will help.

And waiting for him on the other side of the lake were three people who deeply, desperately needed that help.

3. Freedom fighter

What's your greatest achievement? I once played in a soccer match refereed by a World Cup referee. I've met the future king of Great Britain, Prince Charles. And more recently, I had a son (well, my wife did—I watched, which was hard enough). I guess he's probably my greatest achievement, though I'm hoping he doesn't inherit my artistic abilities.

But if I'd ever stood in front of a corpse, said: "Get up," and seen it do as I asked, that would be my greatest achievement. And I'd hope people would hear about it, and go around saying: "You know Carl Laferton? He may be a useless artist, but he can raise people from the dead!"

So the strangest thing about this episode of Original Jesus' life is not what he does for a suffering woman, a grieving father or a dead girl. It's what he says right at the end…

▶ What he really did

When Jesus returned from his trip to the other side of the lake, a crowd welcomed him, for they were all expecting him. Then a man named Jairus, a synagogue leader, came and fell at Jesus' feet, pleading with him to come to his house because his only daughter, a girl of about twelve, was dying.

As Jesus was on his way, the crowds almost crushed him. And a woman was there who had been bleeding for twelve years,

but no one could heal her. She'd spent all she had trying to get her life back; but she was still bleeding, and was now penniless.

So **she came up behind** Jesus **and touched the edge of his cloak, and immediately her bleeding stopped.**

The woman melted back into the crowd. But Jesus stopped. He wanted to see who he had healed.

So, **seeing that she could not go unnoticed,** the woman **came trembling and fell at his feet. She told why she had touched him and how she had been instantly healed. Then he said to her, "Daughter, your faith has healed you. Go in peace."**

While Jesus was still speaking, someone came from the house of Jairus, the synagogue leader. "Your daughter is dead," he said. **"Don't bother the teacher anymore."**

Pausing to speak to this woman had come at a huge cost—a young girl's life.

But Jesus didn't turn sadly away. He **said to Jairus, "Don't be afraid; just believe, and she will be healed."**

When he arrived at the house of Jairus, Jesus went into the house with his disciples **Peter, John and James, and the child's father and mother. All the people were wailing and mourning for** the girl.

"Stop wailing," said Jesus. "She is not dead but asleep."

They laughed at him, knowing that she was dead. Mourning was a group activity in that culture; these people had all seen dead bodies before, and this was a dead body.

But he took her by the hand and said, "My child, get up!"

Her spirit returned, and at once she stood up. Then Jesus told them to give her something to eat. Her parents were astonished, but he ordered them not to tell anyone what had happened.

READ THE FULL STORY Luke 8 v 40-56 and Mark 5 v 26

▶ Why he really matters

When we think of the Romans, we usually think of sandals and togas, straight roads, and Russell Crowe in *Gladiator* (a film I have watched with my eyes open all the way through).

But when Jesus' countrymen, the Jews, thought of Romans, they thought of oppression, unfair taxes, and random killing. That's because, throughout Jesus' life, their land was occupied by a brutal Roman army.

So for the Jews, freedom meant being free of Rome. They dreamed of a freedom fighter who would do the apparently impossible, and release them from the Romans, so that they could live in their land, ruling themselves, in peace.

In our day, many dream of that kind of freedom, too. Millions are being abused by someone else's government, or their own government.

And many people who already enjoy that kind of freedom want more freedom. Freedom from poverty; or from laws they see as unfair; or from paying too much tax. All of us want to be free from something.

So if Jesus is God, if Jesus loves us, and if Jesus really does make a difference, then surely he'll bring us the freedom we want.

Which freedom?

That's what the Jews thought. And that's why Jesus often asked people to keep quiet about the amazing things he did. He knew that when people heard about his power, they'd assume he had come to overpower the Roman armies. They'd demand that he fulfill their dreams of freedom.

And Jesus knew that they'd be disappointed. Not because he hadn't come to bring them freedom, but because he hadn't come to bring *that* freedom. Freedom from the Romans might be the most everyone else dreamed of; but it was a far smaller, less ambitious freedom than he'd come to bring.

Jesus wanted to show them, and he wants to show us, that what he's most interested in is not that kind of here-and-now political or economic or social freedom. It's not that he doesn't care about these things—he does. But he wants to offer a much greater, deeper, more lasting but more elusive freedom.

What is that freedom? It's the freedom we see Jesus offering to that despairing woman and that desperate man and that dead girl.

The slavery of hopelessness

In first-century Israel, if a woman bled continuously instead of once a month it was not only uncomfortable, it was considered shameful. It brought embarrassment and exclusion.

This woman was helpless. Life had gone terribly wrong, and there was nothing she could do about it.

She was in a hopeless situation—and there's not much slavery worse than hopelessness. Maybe you know what it's like to wake up every day with a knot of hopelessness in the pit of your stomach. You have something in common with that woman. Maybe you don't right now, but there've been moments when you've felt that way. You can begin to imagine being that woman.

After all, hopelessness knows no gender, wealth or age boundaries. You can be a poor invalid or an influential mover-and-shaker; a bleeding woman or a synagogue leader. You can't wish, work or buy your way out.

Most of us know what hopelessness is, and how it feels. So we're with the woman as she comes quietly up behind Jesus.

And she's healed. He gives her freedom to be herself, to live and know joy, and look forward. Jesus gives her back her life. He frees her from hopelessness.

It's a wonderful moment.

Except it can't last. There's something worse than hopelessness, which traps us even more securely. Death.

The slavery of death

Death is the greatest trap of all. We spend all of our lives being drawn towards it. It takes away all we've achieved and everything we've accumulated. Death happens; and no politician, president or prince can free us from its grasp.

Except one. To Jesus, giving life to a dead person is like waking a sleeping person. That's what he means when he says: "She is not dead but asleep". Jesus can override the inevitability of death. He can give us life beyond death.

It's easy to think he's joking, or crazy. It's easy to look at the finality of death and think that's one thing we'll never be free of. That's what those mourners were thinking as they "laughed at him". What happened next? Jesus took a very dead girl by the hand, and she became very alive.

Jesus gives her back her life. He frees her from death.

The freedom of the kingdom

As we watch this woman given hope, and this girl given life, Jesus is giving us a glimpse of real freedom: the freedom of life in his kingdom.

God's plan, ever since he made the world, is one day to have a kingdom in the world which stretches around the world. And that kingdom will be a place of total freedom from the things that really oppress us: fear, evil, oppression, regret, illness, and even death.

It's a perfect place. God sets the border controls, and he says anything imperfect will not enter. His kingdom will be a place of complete satisfaction with life and security in life. The hope after hopelessness that we glimpse as this woman is healed, and the life after death that we glimpse as this girl is raised, will one day come fully, completely, for ever.

It's like a visual slogan: *Enjoy the freedom of kingdom life.*

Just imagine for a moment what that kind of life would be like. Freedom from fear, as Jesus showed on the lake. From evil, as he showed on the shore. From embarrassment and hopelessness and grieving and death, as he showed in this town.

This is the life we would all love. In many ways, it's the life we're all trying to build here and now, enjoying brief glimmers of it when we laugh, play, love, achieve, succeed.

As God—as the King of that kingdom—Jesus came to offer this world order. His freedom wasn't about kicking the Romans out in his day, or overthrowing governments, lowering taxes, changing laws and making life fairer in ours. The real Jesus doesn't offer us a blank placard to write our slogans on. The freedom we would ask for may be greater than we can attain, but it's far too small for what he can achieve.

Original Jesus comes to free us from all hopelessness, and even from death, by inviting us into his kingdom. He says: *Enjoy the freedom of kingdom life.* We can start enjoying it now: a life of hope, knowing we have a present with a purpose and a future without fear of death. We can enjoy it supremely in the future: a perfect life in his eternal kingdom.

King Jesus offers freedom with him. He offers us all we need, long for and work for.

And we say... no.

4. Intolerant judge

Picture a courtroom. The trial has lasted several days, and the verdict is due. In the judge's seat is the most senior judge in the land. Facing the verdict is a man accused of stealing millions from his landlord; committing grievous bodily harm against the landlord's employees; and murdering the landlord's son. The accused has pleaded not guilty, but it's the most clear-cut case this judge has ever seen. There's DNA. There's security-camera footage of each crime. There's even a recorded confession.

As the jury file in, the grieving father—the landlord—is in the public gallery to see justice done. The jury foreman rises to give the verdict: "Guilty."

The judge speaks to the criminal.

"You are a thief, a violent man, and a murderer. Your crimes were driven by a hatred of your landlord and a desire to take his place. You deserve to go to prison for a very, very long time—for life. You should never live in that property again.

"However, this is a tolerant society. We don't judge others. So I'll let you go. Off you go. Oh, and you're allowed to carry on living in the property—rent free."

If you read that in the newspaper, you'd be outraged. If you were the parent of the man who was killed, you'd be livid. Why? Because tolerance has its limits. Things like murder are things we won't, and shouldn't, tolerate.

Now imagine that the God of the world was that kind of judge; leaning over to the worst people of our time, or of history, and letting them off with a friendly smile.

I wouldn't want God to be like that. I imagine you wouldn't, either.

Wonderfully, the God we meet in Jesus isn't anything like that.

▶ What he really did

Jesus told the people this story:

"A man planted a vineyard, rented it to some farmers and went away for a long time. At harvest time he sent a servant to the tenants so they would give him some of the fruit of the vineyard as rent.

"But the tenants beat him and sent him away empty-handed.

"So he sent another servant, but that one also they beat and treated shamefully and sent away empty-handed, too. He sent a third, and they wounded him and threw him out.

"Then the owner of the vineyard said, 'What shall I do? I will send my son, whom I love; perhaps they will respect him.'

"But when the tenants saw him, they talked the matter over. 'This is the heir,' they said. 'Let's kill him, and the inheritance will be ours.'

"So they threw him out of the vineyard and killed him.

"What then will the owner of the vineyard do?" asked Jesus.

"He will come and kill those tenants and give the vineyard to others."

READ THE FULL STORY Luke 20 v 9-16

▶ Why he really matters

Ownership argument

In Jesus' story, there's an owner and some tenants. The owner has given the tenants a great vineyard to live in. They can enjoy its produce, as long as they pay their rent.

But these tenants want to be owners. So they use the vineyard for themselves. They reject anyone who reminds them that there's an owner, and it's not them.

And in the end, they kill the owner's son—because then they can live as if they own the vineyard. They'll be free of the real owner, free to run the place for themselves.

These tenants are intolerant. Jesus doesn't tell us how well they treat each other. But he does tell us how intolerant they all are of the owner and his son. They won't let the owner be the owner. They won't let the heir be the heir.

The owner, on the other hand, is very tolerant. If you were these tenants' landlord, at what point would you evict them? When they refused to pay rent? Possibly. When they beat up the guy you sent to collect it? Probably. When they beat up the next two guys you sent? Definitely.

This owner doesn't. In Jesus' story the owner is also the judge, who has the right both to evict them and punish them; and he gives the tenants chance after chance.

But there is one thing he will not tolerate. He won't tolerate what they do to his son. And that's fair enough. Justice must be done. And so, finally, long after I would, the owner-judge steps in. Jesus says: "He will come and kill those tenants."

Good news

Here's the good news. Jesus is telling this story about God. The owner, the judge, is God himself. The vineyard is this world. And the tenants are people who treat this world as though it's their own; as though everything in it is here to enrich and enjoy for themselves or their family or their clan or their country. They're people who steal, and even assault and kill, to get and keep all that they can.

This is a world full of injustice: of people doing awful things and getting away with it. Maybe you or a loved one has been (or is being) a victim, and whoever did it hasn't had to answer or pay for what they did. You long for justice, you feel you need justice, but you don't see justice.

It will come. God is a judge who won't tolerate wrongdoing for ever. He'll judge it and he'll punish it. You will get justice.

There's a very common view that the God of the Bible is judgmental and intolerant. Someone recently put it very well on a website called agnosticreview.com: "Peel away the fluffy portions of Jesus, and an intolerant zealot is exposed." Instinctively, we don't like this idea of God—because judging others is wrong, and intolerance is bad.

Well, Jesus was very clear that this is exactly who he is—he is an intolerant judge. The surprise, though, is that this is exactly who we want him to be, what we need him to be. Actually, God judges what we want him to judge; he is intolerant of what we really want him not to tolerate.

Strange as it may seem, God's intolerance is great news.

Troubling news

But it's also troubling news. Everything those tenants do is driven by one central attitude: a rejection of the owner. And that rejection is seen most of all, and worst of all, in how they treat the owner's son.

In reality, the owner is God. So who does the "son" in the story represent?

It's Jesus.

We need to take a bit of a diversion here. How can Jesus be both God—the God who controls the weather in a storm—*and* his Son?! This is a little insight into who God is, and always has been through eternity. He is one God, in three persons. Each of those three is fully God, and each is different. God is the Father (who we tend to call "God"); the Son (who we usually call "Jesus"); and the Holy Spirit.

I can't get my head around this! But that's OK—it would actually be disappointing if I could fully understand everything about God, because my human mind is limited. God the Father, Son and Spirit is far deeper, and more interesting, than a made-up god. He's far bigger than our brains can handle. That's exciting!

But it's also challenging; because it means that if we reject the son, we are rejecting the owner; if we reject Jesus as God's Son, we reject God.

The worst crime anyone can commit—the crime that stands behind all other crimes, great and small—is living as though God is not God. The worst thing anyone can do is to say to Jesus: "You are not God's Son, you are not my King, and I will live as though you're not. I will not tolerate you."

The Bible has a word for that attitude—sin.

Sin and me

When I'm honest with myself, I know my instinctive attitude is to sin. I don't kill Jesus (I was brought up with manners and morals). So I sin much more politely than those tenants.

I simply change Jesus. In my head, I re-draw him into an image I want. I let him be a good teacher to advise me, when I agree with him. I let him be a friend, when he seems good to know. I ask for his help, when I have a problem.

But I will not accept Jesus' actual identity: the Son of God, the one who has the right to tell me how to live in his world. I'm a tenant who wants to be an owner. I'm a sinner.

Sin and us

The hard truth is that, deep down, we're all like that. So we take what is rightfully God's and use it for ourselves. We don't beat up people who warn us, but we do ignore them, and sometimes laugh at them. We may not murder his Son, but we kill him off in our hearts each time we say: "I will not let you be who you are, Jesus." We reject the freedom of life with Jesus, of living with him as King, so that we can be free of Jesus, living however we want.

And this leaves us facing the justice that we cry out for. God's intolerance of wrongdoing is great news for us when we suffer; it is terrifying news for us because we sin. God is not going to lean over from his judge's chair and say to us: "You ignored me. You killed off my Son. But don't worry—I'll forget about justice; I'll tolerate what you never would; I'll ignore your crime."

And the punishment fits the crime. We don't want Jesus to be King, so we won't live in his kingdom. We'll be evicted: shut out of enjoying a life of which the best we have here is just a glimpse. Instead, we'll experience an existence outside that kingdom, of which the worst of this life is merely a glimmer, in a place Jesus called "hell."

None of us will pass through the border control into Jesus' kingdom.

A way out

And yet there is a way out. The story should finish with the tenants being evicted. But it doesn't. Jesus adds something very strange. The owner will "give the vineyard to others."

There is still a way into the kingdom of freedom and perfection we all long for. How does anyone get in? The answer Jesus gave to that question is perhaps the most misunderstood, controversial and offensive anyone has ever given.

5. Religious rule-keeper

Last year, for the first time, I flew from the UK to the US. The guys on border control don't mess about. If your paperwork isn't all in order, you are firmly encouraged to hop on a plane back to the UK.

It should be nerve-racking... except you already know you'll get in, because you apply for permission to enter beforehand, over the internet. You get the verdict emailed to you weeks before you land in America, and that verdict shows up on the border control computers. Deep down, you know the guy on passport control will let you in.

The most important border control in eternity is the one for Jesus' perfect kingdom. And, since we're all tenants who act like we're owners, none of us deserve to be let through. But there is a way to be allowed in—and in this story, Jesus told his listeners how they could know for sure whether they'd be let through, or turned away.

❯ What he really did

To some who were confident of their own righteousness and looked down on everyone else, Jesus told this story:

"Two men went up to the temple in Jerusalem **to pray, one a Pharisee**—a religious leader—**the other a tax collector**—a Jewish traitor who worked for the Romans.

"The Pharisee stood by himself and prayed: 'God, I thank you that I am not like other people—robbers, evildoers, adulterers—or even like this tax collector. I fast twice a week and give a tenth of all I get.'

"But the tax collector stood at a distance. He would not even look up to heaven, but, as a sign of mourning, beat his breast and said, 'God, have mercy on me, a sinner.'

"I tell you that this man, rather than the other, went home justified before God. For all those who exalt themselves will be humbled, and those who humble themselves will be exalted."

READ THE FULL STORY Luke 18 v 9-14

❯ Why he really matters

Jesus' story involves two men. One of the two ends up "justified"— declared not guilty of any crime—by God. He finishes the story "righteous"—right with God, able to enter his perfect kingdom.

So which man is it? Let's meet the candidates.

On the one hand, we have one of the most religious men imaginable. He takes keeping God's rules seriously, and he's good at it. He has a religious job. He fasts twice a week. He gives money away. He has avoided making the mistakes that loads of people around him make—whether it's in public, in his heart, or in his bed, he's doing well. He's trying very hard to be a good tenant.

In our terms, this Pharisee is a very, very good and well-respected pastor, whose private life is as blameless as his public life.

The other man is a treacherous outcast. Tax collectors were hated. They ignored God's law so that they could work for the Romans and take other people's money as their own, by overcharging on tax. The money they raised paid for swords for Romans and luxuries for themselves. We don't really have an equivalent in our society, but think of a conman who preys on vulnerable old ladies and sells state secrets to North Korea, and you're not far off.

So here they are: the Pharisee and the tax collector. The pastor and the conman. The do-gooder and the messed-up.

Which of them gets in?

The pastor?

There's an image of Jesus that is very popular with churchgoing people, moral people, good people. This Jesus—Religious Rule-keeping Jesus—has a very simple message: if you're good, God will be good to you. He divides the world into two: good people, and bad people—and if you've kept the rules your church or society lays out, you're welcomed into his kingdom.

So, as Religious Rule-keeping Jesus looks at these two men, he says to the pastor: "Come on in. You've been really good. You're going home justified. You'll pass straight through passport control and into the kingdom. Hey, we'll roll out the red carpet for a guy like you."

And then he turns to the conman and says: "No way. Look at your life. Don't even bother turning up."

Everyone listening to the real Jesus as he told this story was fully expecting him to say that. They were "confident of their own righteousness." They were rule-keeping people. They knew they were better than lots of other people (like tax collectors). They knew that God is good to good people.

I haven't done any scientific analysis to back up this claim, but I think most people today are "confident of their own righteousness". They've decided which rules they need to keep in order to qualify as "good," and they know they're keeping them. It may include going to church, and keeping the Ten Commandments—being obviously "religious." Or it may mean bringing up your kids well, mowing an elderly neighbor's lawn, and not fiddling your expenses or taking extra time at lunchbreak—simply being "good."

Very simply, if we think God will be good to us because we've been good, then we're "confident of our own righteousness."

If that's you, you'll love Religious Rule-keeping Jesus.

So the real Jesus is about to shock you...

This is offensive

Because here's what Original Jesus said. Talking about the tax collector, the conman, he said:

"I tell you that this man went home justified."

Jesus says the rule-breaker, the lowlife who cheats and betrays and steals, is in—headed for his kingdom.

And that's not all—he added: "This man, rather than the other, went home justified."

This is the verdict. We know what will happen at the border of the kingdom of God. The conman will be welcomed in. The pastor will be turned away.

This is really offensive! Think of the worst person you know. They can get eternal perfection. Think of the very best person you know. They might not.

What is going on?

The difference

The difference that really matters—the difference that will matter for all eternity—is not between the pastor and the conman's goodness. It's between their approach.

The pastor approaches God offering all he's done. He knows he's good. The conman approaches offering nothing. He knows he's bad.

What makes all the difference is that the conman admits he doesn't deserve to get in—he calls himself "a sinner"—while the pastor thinks he does deserve to. The conman simply asks for a place in the kingdom, while the pastor doesn't think of asking, because he assumes he already has a place.

Jesus doesn't divide the world into good and bad people. That's because his kingdom isn't just good—a place we're allowed into if our positives outweigh our negatives. His kingdom is perfect—any negatives leave us outside.

So to deserve a place in Jesus' kingdom, the Pharisee would need to be perfect. He'd need to be as good as God is. And notice that he doesn't compare himself with God. If he did, he'd be like the tax collector, who won't even look at God because he knows how useless he is compared to him. No—the Pharisee compares himself to "other people."

If we compare ourselves to others, and find some who are worse than us, we can convince ourselves we're good enough. When we compare ourselves to God, and recognise we're considerably worse than him, we have to accept that we can never be good enough.

Imagine Marie Childs, the art champion of my class, turning up to the Metropolitan Museum of Art in New York with a drawing she's done of her mother and saying: "You'll hang this in your main gallery, of course. I'm a better artist than everyone else in my school, particularly Carl Laferton—he can't draw at all." That's what it's like to approach the perfect God and say: "You'll let me into your kingdom. I'm a good person—much better than most other people I know."

Everyone and anyone

In reality, the division isn't between good and bad. It's between people who don't ask, and people who do.

This is very challenging for people who, like me, think of themselves as "good." No-one's goodness will get them into the life we all want. Everyone needs to ask.

And it's very exciting for people who, like the tax collector, are honest about themselves; for people who know they're not very good, perhaps compared to others, and certainly compared to God. It's exciting because no one's lack of goodness stops them getting into the kingdom life we all want.

Everyone needs to ask; and everyone can ask.

I was once walking through a town in northern England. Just in front of me, two women met one another. "Are you going in there?!" one of them asked the other, motioning to a nearby church.

"No, of course I'm not!" said the other woman. "They wouldn't have me."

Neither would Religious, Rule-keeping Jesus.

Original Jesus would. Original Jesus does.

A problem

This would be a great place to finish the chapter. But there's a problem. Since God is a just God—since he is intolerant of sin—how can he simply let a sinner like this tax collector in, without them doing anything except asking?

The answer to that question isn't found in Jesus' life, miracles, teaching or story-telling... but in his death.

6. Tragic failure

Perhaps because I was useless at art, I became (and still am) a bit of a history geek. I loved reading about the battles, the alliances, the struggles, the stories of rags-to-riches and riches-to-rags.

Most of history has been brutal—particularly if you tried to reach the top. It was all or nothing. So in 1066, two men landed in England with large armies, each confident of taking the crown of England from King Harold. The first, Hardrada, was defeated, and died on the battlefield. The second, William, was victorious, and ruled for 21 years as "the Conqueror."

Throughout history, you won or you lost. The stakes were high, the rewards were great… but the fall was total, painful, and final.

And Jesus lost. Only five days after entering the capital, Jerusalem, and being welcomed as a king, Jesus left it again as a condemned criminal. He rode in on a donkey, just as great Jewish rulers had done centuries before; he left it saddled with a cross, walking towards his death.

> What he really did

When they came to the place called the Skull, they crucified Jesus there, along with the criminals—one on his right, the other on his left.

The people stood watching, and the religious **rulers even sneered at him.** Just days before, he had been challenging their right to make the rules, threatening their power, and warning that being proudly religious wasn't the way into God's kingdom.

But now, those leaders had had the last laugh. They'd arrested Jesus late at night. They'd convicted him in a show trial, and convinced the Roman governor to execute him. In a few hours, they would be rid of Jesus.

One of the criminals who hung there hurled insults at him: "Aren't you the King? **Save yourself and us!"**

But the other criminal rebuked him. "Don't you fear God," he said, **"since you are under the same sentence? We are punished justly, for we are getting what our deeds deserve.**

"But this man has done nothing wrong."

Then he said, "Jesus, remember me when you come into your kingdom."

Jesus answered him, "Truly I tell you, today you will be with me in paradise."

It was now about noon, and darkness came over the whole land until three in the afternoon, for the sun stopped shining. This wasn't some kind of natural eclipse—the timing was wrong for that. It was strange… and it was significant. As the Jews who were watching knew, God had already explained it. Centuries before, he had warned them—his people, who he'd lived with, looked after and spoken to—that he wouldn't go on putting up with their sin, with their determination to live as owners rather than tenants.

He had told them a day was coming when his punishment would come—a day that they would be thrown out of the vineyard of his world. He'd take away all the good things they'd enjoyed from him without ever thinking of or thanking him—including life itself.

God had said it would be pretty obvious when it came: **"In that day, I will make the sun go down at noon and darken the earth in broad daylight."**

Now, as his Son hung on the cross, God's punishment, eviction day, had come.

And yet, apart from the darkness, everything seemed normal. Perhaps it was a false alarm!

Then **Jesus called out with a loud voice, "Father, into your hands I commit my spirit." When he had said this, he breathed his last.**

The Roman **centurion** who had been overseeing the executions, **seeing what had happened, praised God and said, "Surely this was a righteous,** innocent **man."**

The people beat their breasts, the traditional acknowledgement that someone had died, **and went away. The women who had followed him from Galilee stood at a distance, watching these things.**

But there was nothing left to see. Innocent or not, the man who'd claimed to be a king had breathed his last. The show was over. Jesus was dead.

READ THE FULL STORY Luke 23 v 33-49 and Amos 8 v 9-14

> Why he really matters

Riches to rags

For all Jesus' talk and teaching, for all his great promises and miracles, he failed. Tragically, his great vision of a kingdom of perfection and freedom was crushed by the cold reality of political power and military might.

Jesus played the game, and he lost. As the world religions section at London's Millennium Dome exhibition put it: "Jesus died tragically young." Just another of history's footnotes. Another loser, mocked by the winners as he died.

It was a total defeat. And that wasn't even the worst of it. There was something more devastating happening. We don't see it by looking around the cross at the laughter and scorn, but by looking above Jesus' cross at the midday darkness.

This darkness was the sign that God's punishment for sin had come. Eviction day was here. Of course it was! Wouldn't you want justice if your son was killed? It was time for the tenants who had kicked out God's Son to be kicked out themselves.

And yet, during the darkness, the tenants didn't die. Only one person did—God's Son. It was Jesus who was evicted by his Father. Even God was rejecting him.

So this is the ultimate story of riches-to-rags. This man was God the Son, who had lived eternally in his kingdom with his Father, enjoying perfect friendship with him. This man was Jesus of Nazareth, who had done so much for, and promised so much to, people. And now he was dying, scorned by people and rejected by his Father.

If you've ever looked at the cross and thought: at the end of the day, Jesus failed… you're right.

Rags to riches

But not everyone looked at Jesus and laughed.

One man—a serious criminal, whose actions had earned him the death penalty—spoke to the man dying next to him.

What did he spend several of his precious last breaths saying? He *admitted to something*. Speaking of himself and the other criminal, he said: "We are getting what our deeds deserve." He knew he should "fear God," the God he had rejected all his life and was now about to meet. He knew that the agony of his death was not the end of his suffering, but the beginning.

And then he *asked for something*, something outrageous for a man whose life had been so rotten that he'd been justly condemned to death: "Jesus, remember me when you come into your kingdom."

Somehow, he knew Jesus was king of a kingdom beyond death; and he wanted Jesus to give him a place there.

Like the conman in that story Jesus told, this criminal admitted his own wrongdoing, and he asked for a place in the kingdom. And Jesus answered:

"Truly I tell you, today you will be with me in paradise."

This man's death, Jesus said, would not be a dead-end—the end of any snatches of joy or contentment he found in his brutal life. It would be a doorway to paradise, to the kingdom. These men met at the worst place imaginable; they could continue getting to know each other in the best.

Jesus lost everything on the cross. His riches were replaced by rags. But that criminal won everything on the cross. His rags would turn to riches later that day.

Rags taken, riches given

These two men dying on their crosses show us how Jesus has opened the way into his kingdom.

Jesus, as that criminal realized, had "done nothing wrong." He, alone of all the people there that day, alone of all the people who have ever lived, deserved to enjoy kingdom life. But instead, he died like a tenant. Jesus died the death of a sinner, judged by his Father.

He died the criminal's death.

This is what Jesus was doing on the cross. Taking the criminal's sin on himself, taking the punishment that sin deserved, taking the sinful rags from the other man and dying in his place. And giving the criminal his riches; giving him eternal kingdom life.

Jesus lost everything so that he could give everything. His death wasn't primarily a mistake, or a failure, or even really a tragedy. It was why he came to earth. As Jesus told his friends months before, he "must be killed" (Luke 9 v 22).

When Jesus calmed the storm, conquered the demons, healed the bleeding lady, raised the dead girl and challenged the rule-keeping religious people, he knew he was walking towards his own death. He knew he was headed for a cross where he would take the rags of sin from, and give his riches of kingdom life to, anyone who asks. He loved people—loved you—enough to go to his death to offer us life.

His greatest defeat was also his greatest victory.

Dead promises

But… dying men say all sorts of things, even ones who claim to be kings. The promise of a dying man is worth nothing. Dead men can't keep their word, and dead kings can't rule.

And death won. Jesus lost.

But death only won for three days. Those women who had followed Jesus, and witnessed his total defeat, also witnessed his final victory.

Three days after Jesus' lifeless body had been hauled off a cross, and three days after the women saw **his body laid in a tomb,** they got up **very early in the morning,** and **took the spices they had prepared and went to the tomb.** In a hot country, the smell of corpses was horrendous, so spices were used to mask the stench.

But there was no corpse to rub them into.

They found the stone rolled away from the tomb. But when they entered, they did not find the body of the Lord Jesus.

While they were wondering about this, suddenly two men in clothes that gleamed like lightning—angels—stood beside them.

"Why do you look for the living among the dead?" the men said. **"He is not here; he has risen!"** *

Dying men say all sorts of things. But none then rise back to life so that they can keep their promises. Jesus did. He returned from beyond death to show that he had defeated death.

Death lost. Jesus won.

On the Friday, he had looked like a failure and was treated as a failure. But that wasn't the end of the story. On the Sunday, Jesus was revealed as the ultimate victor. He took others' rags to give them his riches; then he rose to share in those riches.

Jesus has offered that take-and-give relationship ever since. The story is going on today—and it includes us.

Three views

Everyone today makes something of the man on the middle cross that day. To most, Jesus is an irrelevance, just as he was to the people who gathered to see him die, and then wandered off to get on with their lives. To some, Jesus is an object of ridicule, as he was to the rulers who laughed at his failure. But to others, like that criminal, Jesus is the loving rescuer—dying to hold out kingdom life, taking their rags to offer his riches.

Everyone makes something of this man. Who do *you* see on that cross?

* READ THE FULL STORY Luke 23 v 55 – 24 v 6

7. Children's story

The Bible is right up there in my two-year-old's list of favorite books—along with a tense drama about a cat who loses his owner, and a gripping account of a mouse's bedtime routine. Benjamin likes turning to the page with a picture of the baby Jesus lying in a manger with a sheep and a cow looking at him.

Jesus is a great story for children. He provides them with Christmas (ie: presents) and Easter (ie: chocolate eggs), and with a friend to talk to all year round.

And then we grow up, we learn about the real world, and we leave children's stories behind (though we hang onto the presents and the eggs). So we leave Jesus behind, too.

> What he really did

As he approached Jerusalem, **people were bringing babies to Jesus for him to place his hands on them. When the disciples saw this, they** scolded them. This was the Son of God, the ultimate king, a miracle-working, freedom-offering teacher. This was not a kindergarten teacher. Jesus had more important things to do and more important people to see.

But Jesus called the children to him and said, "Let the little children come to me, and do not hinder them, for the kingdom of God belongs to such as these.

"Truly I tell you, anyone who will not receive the kingdom of God like a little child will never enter it."

READ THE FULL STORY Luke 18 v 15-17

❯ Why he really matters

In many ways, it would be easier if Jesus were just a story for our children. You don't need to take a children's story seriously. You don't need to let it change and challenge you. No one has built their life around *The Hungry Caterpillar*. No one outside the land of Fairy-Tale ever said to Prince Charming: "You are my king, and I'll live for you."

So there's probably something deep within us that would quite like to hold onto an image of Children's Story Jesus. But what does the real Jesus say? Is he for kids?

Original Jesus says: "Kind of."

First, he's a true story. It really happened. He really lived. And his resurrection, on a particular day in human history, proves who he really was.

Second, he did come for children, to say to them: "Enjoy the freedom of kingdom life."

So it does look as though Jesus is saying that he's here for children. After all, he himself looks at these children and says: "The kingdom of God belongs to these."

Except that's not quite what Jesus says. He adds two crucial words:

"The kingdom of God belongs to *such as* these."

Those two words capture the reason Jesus came, lived, died and rose. They describe how you and I can know we have a place in his kingdom; how we can enjoy freedom from fear and hopelessness and death; how we can be sure that God is for us, and not against us.

Jesus isn't saying he's come only for children. He's saying he's come for anyone who is child-like.

That's not the same as childish. He's not asking us to throw a tantrum in the mall, refuse to eat our vegetables, or draw pictures of people who have arms growing out of their heads.

Child-like people are simply people who are willing to relate to Jesus as a child relates to a parent—to come to him, and receive from him.

Come to me

Young children are by nature curious. They want to know new things. They're very good at changing their minds about things when they need to, because they know they don't know everything. They ask questions and listen to truth.

As we grow up, we find all those things harder. We're less able to change our minds; we don't like to admit we might be wrong on something, or we don't understand; we stop asking questions if we might not like the answer; when truth hurts, we look for ways to ignore or reshape it.

Jesus invites us to come to him, get to know him, learn from him, and treat him as who he is: God's Son, our King. He invites us to enjoy the certainty of knowing what life is all about; the confidence that comes from knowing how to live. He challenges us to reshape our lives under his loving rule, by accepting that he knows better than us—that he's God and we're tenants, that he's in charge.

It's great to be able come to King Jesus. It means that the person in charge of your life is someone who knows everything about life (ie: not you!). It means that the Holy Spirit—God himself—comes to live in you, to help, guide, comfort and support you. It's great to come to King Jesus—but it's hard, too, because it requires being child-like.

Receive from me

When a young child wants something, they look for their nearest parent (or, failing that, someone else's parent), and just ask. If they want some food, they don't try to pay for it themselves, or claim they deserve it. They just ask. They simply trust that they'll be given what they need.

Asking is all a child can do, and all a child needs to do.

Throughout his life, Jesus gave glimpses of what life in his future kingdom will be like. It will be calm and without fear. It will be empty of evil and full of joy. There will be freedom from everything that right now makes your life less good than you'd like it to be. It will be perfect: better than the best day you can imagine.

And in his life and death, Jesus opened the way into his kingdom. He has done everything necessary to take the rags of our sin and give us the riches of his perfection. He invites us to have kingdom life for ever, by being people "such as" children—people who admit they can't get in on their own, and so they ask for a place.

When we come to Jesus as the King and trust that he has opened the way into his kingdom, we receive life in that kingdom from him.

Which Jesus?

I can still remember the evening nearly 14 years ago when I realized my mental sketch of Jesus was not the real one, not the right one. It was a shock, because I thought I had life sorted, and suddenly I didn't. And it was unsettling, because I'd always thought I was headed for his heavenly kingdom, and I suddenly understood that I wasn't.

I hadn't been coming to Jesus as King. I'd changed him to suit myself. I hadn't been receiving from Jesus. I'd assumed I'd be fine, that I was good enough.

And here was Original Jesus.

He wasn't a made-up story—he had lived in human history. I couldn't change him—I needed to let him change me. I couldn't rule him—

I needed to let him rule me. And I wasn't good enough—I needed to admit that, and ask him to take my sin and the judgment I deserve, and trust him to give me a place in his kingdom.

I did the only sensible thing to do. I came to Jesus as my King, and received from him life with him. And, looking back, while it made my life harder in so many ways, it has also made life much more exciting, satisfying and fulfilling. And ahead of me lies a guaranteed place in his perfect kingdom.

Maybe as you've read this book, you've come to the same realization as I did. Your version of Jesus doesn't really match the real one.

It might be, as you finish reading this book, that you need to do some more thinking, ask some questions, do some research, to work out for yourself who Original Jesus really was, and is. Over the page, there are a few ways you could do that.

But perhaps you know who the Original Jesus, the Jesus of history, is. And you've realized you need to come to him as your King, and receive a place in his kingdom from him.

There's nothing you have done that is so bad that you can't ask for a place in his kingdom. There's nothing you have done that is so good that you don't need to ask.

Why not speak to him now?

What next?

Thanks for reading this book. I hope you've enjoyed it, and that it's informed and even excited you about Jesus.

I'm guessing you fall into one of two categories:

Maybe you're **someone who would like to keep looking into Christianity** before making your mind up about what you believe. Here are a few ways you can keep thinking things through...

Read a Gospel. There are four historical biographies of Jesus' life found in the Bible—Matthew, Mark, Luke and John (this book has mainly used parts of Luke). Why not grab one and read through it? The shortest one is Mark, which takes around two hours to read.

Pray. That may seem strange! But why not speak to God, and ask him, if he is there, to help you to see the truth about who he is, who Jesus is, and what life is all about?

Go to a website. *www.christianityexplored.org* allows you to keep thinking about Jesus in your own way, at your own pace, in your own time. It features an animation which explains who Jesus is, why he came, and what it means for us; some video answers to questions lots of people ask; and some real-life stories of people who thought things through themselves. And on the site, you can also find out about how you can...

Join a Christianity Explored course. This is an informal, relaxed, seven-week walk through the Gospel of Mark, where you can ask questions, discuss, or simply listen. You can find a course near you on the website.

Look at the historical evidence. If you'd like to look in more detail at how we know that the Gospels are real history, a great book to read is *The Case for Christ*, by Lee Strobel.

Maybe, though, you're reading this page as *someone who has come to Jesus as King and received a place in his kingdom from him*—you've become a Christian. That's fantastic! It can all seem a bit strange at first (or at least, it did for me). The best advice I can give you is to **find a church** near you that bases all it says on the Bible (in the same way this book does). The people there will help you get on with enjoying knowing Jesus, your Ruler and Rescuer, and encourage you to see how you can worship him. If you'd like a hand with finding a church like this, just email info@thegoodbook.com

Yes, but...
isn't this all made up?

When you read something, it helps to know what you're reading. I wouldn't use a car manual to tell me how to cook a roast dinner; I wouldn't use a recipe book to help me change my car's oil!

Throughout this book, you'll have seen me talking about what the four "Gospels" in the Bible tell us about Jesus. And I talk about what they say as though those things really happened; as though they were history. Why?

Because that's the type of books the Gospels are. Here's how one of the four, the one written by a man called Luke, begins:

Many have undertaken to draw up an account of the things that have been fulfilled among us, just as they were handed down to us by those who from the first were eye-witnesses and servants of the word.

With this in mind, since I myself have carefully investigated everything from the beginning, I too decided to write an orderly account for you, most excellent Theophilus, so that you may know the certainty of the things you have been taught.

Luke was writing his Gospel about Jesus for someone he knew, a guy called Theophilus. And what he wanted to do was to let Theophilus know what had actually happened to Jesus. He'd researched it all; he'd spoken to eye-witnesses who'd seen what really happened; and now he'd written it all out in an "orderly" way.

He was writing a historical biography of Jesus' life. That's his claim.

Now of course, Luke could have just made it all up, just as I could rewrite history to make my dad an NBA star instead of a retired computing teacher. But it's completely unlikely that Luke would have done that, for two reasons.

First, at the time Luke and the other Gospel authors were writing their historical biographies of Jesus, you could very easily get killed for being a Christian. Why make up something that could land you in prison, facing torture and death?! It would be like me making up a back-story for my dad which claimed that he was a high-level al-Qaeda terrorist, and that I was working for him.

Second, Luke was a Christian. It's easy to think that'd make it more likely that he'd make his Gospel up. Actually, it makes it less likely. If Luke thought this guy Jesus was God, he'd really, really care about getting the facts about him correct. He wouldn't want to make mistakes about someone so important. He'd be more careful to tell historical fact, not less.

One final thing that can make us even more confident that Luke and the others are telling us historical facts is that their stories fit with other historical accounts of the time. The events they talk about fit with other histories. The people they talk about, like Roman emperors and Jewish priests, are real people. Jesus himself is mentioned by both Roman and Jewish historians who would probably rather he hadn't lived; so he himself definitely existed. And the details of the places they wrote about, like how there were two towns next to each other with the same name, check out with archaeological research.

Which means that the Gospels claim to be historical fact; they sound like historical fact; and they check out with other histories as historical fact. Which is why, in this book, I treat what they say about Jesus as historical fact. Strange facts, amazing facts, challenging facts, but still facts!

If you'd like to think in more detail about why we can be confident that the Gospels are history, a couple of great books to read are: *Can we trust what the Gospels say about Jesus?* (published by Matthias Media) or *The Case for Christ* (published by Zondervan).

Yes, but...
can we really believe in miracles?

You don't have to read a Gospel (or this book) for long before you come across a miracle—an event that science can't explain, and which seems to break the normal "rules"—such as a storm being stilled by a word, or a dead girl being raised back to life.

And that gives many of us a problem—because we don't believe in miracles. The world always works in ways that can be explained, and scientific laws are never broken. So how can anyone with brains conclude that miracles can happen?

Well, it all depends on where you start, because where you start affects where you finish, what you conclude. When it comes to miracles, we all start with one of three assumptions:

1. Science can explain everything—miracles cannot happen.

2. Miracles do happen—and anything I can't explain is a miracle.

3. Scientific laws usually explain things—but miracles might happen; I'm unsure.

If I start at option one, then when I come across Jesus seeming to do a miracle, I will immediately say that the Gospel is wrong, without considering the evidence. That's because I'm assuming that there isn't a God who does things I can't explain. It doesn't matter how much evidence there might be—where I've started ("Miracles do not happen") dictates where I finish.

Equally, if I start at option two, then when I come across things in life I can't explain, I will immediately call them "miracles," without considering the evidence. That's because I'm assuming that there isn't a scientific explanation for anything that I don't immediately understand. Where I've started completely dictates where I finish.

But if I start at option three, then as I go through life, and as I read a Gospel, I'll expect things to work according to scientific laws. But I'll also be open to the fact that there could be a God who works through miracles—and I'll be open to following where the evidence takes me.

Actually, option three is the most open-minded. And so, as we read a Gospel and come across apparent "miracles," it's worth neither assuming that miracles happen all the time (whenever I can't explain something), nor that miracles can never happen (because science explains everything). Which means that something that looks like a miracle, sounds like a miracle and claims to be a miracle could well be a miracle.

After all, if there's a God who invented all the laws of science, and if that God came to live on earth as a man, he himself wouldn't be limited by those laws. And ultimately, the only way to prove who he was would be to show that those laws don't limit him.

So, if Jesus is God, then we shouldn't write him off because he does amazing things that we can't get our heads around. In fact, we should expect him to do stuff that is bigger, better and more mind-blowing than we could ever explain or manage!

Yes, but...
surely Jesus didn't really rise?

One of Jesus' earliest followers, Paul, wrote that: **"If Christ has not been raised ... faith is useless."** *

The resurrection of Jesus back to life is the place where the whole of Christianity stands or falls. And the resurrection of Jesus is the place where lots of people say: "That's just ridiculous. The rest of the story, OK—but not a dead man coming back to life!"

Let's be clear. No one can prove beyond any doubt that Jesus rose from the dead. But that's because no one can prove anything beyond any doubt. I can't prove my wife loves me—but, based on the evidence, I believe that she does. You can't prove that you're not a butterfly who's dreaming it's a human—but, based on the evidence, you believe that you're not (hopefully!).

So in thinking about whether Jesus rose or not, it's about what you think is the *most likely* explanation for what happened that day in history.

And people have come up with some pretty good explanations. Over the page are the best I've found. For each, I've laid out the explanation as well as I can, and then mentioned the questions that they don't really answer.

* 1 Corinthians 15 v 17 *(New English Translation Bible version)*

1. There was no empty tomb: the women went to the wrong one

The women were tired and upset when they saw where Jesus was laid. When they visited the body a couple of days later, they went to the wrong tomb. The body wasn't there, they put two and two together and made 648, and told everyone he'd been raised.

Unanswered questions:

- They weren't expecting him to rise. If you went to the wrong tomb, wouldn't you just find the right one, not announce a resurrection?!

- When Jesus' followers announced a month or so later that Jesus had risen, why didn't the authorities simply go to the tomb they'd put soldiers outside, get the body, and disprove the resurrection?

2. The tomb was empty because Jesus wasn't really dead

Jesus didn't die on the cross—he just fainted, and then came round in the cool tomb. He then spent time with his friends and ate and walked with them, and then went away and lived somewhere else. His friends assumed he'd gone to heaven, and started talking about the resurrection.

Unanswered questions:

- The Romans were good at crucifying people. Did they really think Jesus was dead when he wasn't?

- One of the soldiers near the cross stuck a spear into his side. Could a man who'd been stabbed in the heart survive without medical help for three days and then walk out?

- Could a man who'd been nailed to a cross go for a long walk with friends two days later?

- Why didn't the guards at the tomb notice Jesus limping out?

3. The tomb was empty because the body was taken by the authorities

The leaders knew Jesus had predicted his resurrection. So they moved the body to make sure there could be no scam. That left an empty tomb; and the disciples took advantage of this, or misunderstood this, and went round saying Jesus had risen.

Unanswered questions:

• If the authorities had the body, why didn't they produce it when people started believing Jesus had risen? That would have stopped the rumors of resurrection!

4. The tomb was empty because the body was taken by grave-robbers

Bodies weren't valuable, but grave-clothes were. So some grave-robbers stole the body. The tomb was left empty for the women to find, and a legend was born.

Unanswered questions:

• Why, when the empty tomb was discovered, were the valuable grave-clothes still there? Why hadn't the grave-robbers taken the only thing in the tomb of value?

5. The tomb was empty because the body was taken by the disciples

Jesus' followers had much to gain from a "resurrection". So they stole the body, announced the resurrection and said Jesus had appeared to them several times, and that he'd now gone away again, back to heaven. And the resurrection lie enabled them to set up a new religion—Christlanity.

Unanswered questions:

• Could the disciples, who were terrified and had run away when Jesus was arrested, really have managed to pull off stealing a body from under the noses of some Roman guards?

- If the disciples had made up the Gospels of Jesus in the Bible, why do they come across in them as scared, disloyal and weak? Wouldn't you write more impressive lies about yourself?

- If the disciples made this up, they knew for a fact Jesus hadn't risen. Yet almost all of them ended up being killed for saying he'd come back to life and was God. Wouldn't at least one of them have admitted it was all made up to avoid being crucified, stoned to death, or beheaded?

6. The disciples didn't really see Jesus: it was a hallucination

The "appearances" of Jesus were simple hallucinations. After all, the disciples were emotional, tired and grieving—and they saw what they wanted to see.

Unanswered questions:

- Medically, people simply don't hallucinate the same thing at the same time. Did dozens (and on one occasion hundreds) of adults really have an identical hallucination at the same time?

- Why was the tomb empty? If this was a hallucination, the body would still have been in the tomb.

7. The tomb was empty because Jesus had risen back to life

This is what Jesus' friends claimed had happened, even when they faced gruesome deaths for saying it. It explains the empty tomb; and it explains the appearances of Jesus after his death.

Unanswered questions:

- Do people really rise from the dead? It's not exactly a normal event! (To which my answer, for what it's worth, is that if you were God, you could raise someone from the dead without difficulty. And if you wanted to prove you were God, you'd need to do something amazing and abnormal—like promising to die and rise again, and then actually doing that.)

Original Jesus
US edition
© The Good Book Company 2014.

The Good Book Company
Email: info@thegoodbook.com

Websites:
North America: www.thegoodbook.com
UK: www.thegoodbook.co.uk
Australia: www.thegoodbook.com.au
New Zealand: www.thegoodbook.co.nz

All Scripture Quotations, unless otherwise indicated, are taken from the Holy Bible: New International Version ®. Copyright © 2011 by International Bible Society. Used by permission of Zondervan Publishing House. All rights reserved. No part of this publication may be reproduced, stored in a retrieval system, or transmitted on any form or by any means—electronic, mechanical, photocopy, recording, or any other—except for brief quotations in printed reviews, without the prior permission of the publisher.

ISBN: 9781909559837

Design by André Parker
Printed in the US

thegoodbook
COMPANY
Opening up the Bible

At The Good Book Company, we are dedicated to helping Christians and local churches grow. We believe that God's growth process always starts with hearing clearly what he has said to us through his timeless word—the Bible.

Ever since we opened our doors in 1991, we have been striving to produce resources that honor God in the way the Bible is used. We have grown to become an international provider of user-friendly resources to the Christian community, with believers of all backgrounds and denominations using our Bible studies, books, evangelistic resources, DVD-based courses and training events.

We want to equip ordinary Christians to live for Christ day by day, and churches to grow in their knowledge of God, their love for one another, and the effectiveness of their outreach.

Call us for a discussion of your needs or visit one of our local websites for more information on the resources and services we provide.

North America: www.thegoodbook.com
UK & Europe: www.thegoodbook.co.uk
Australia: www.thegoodbook.com.au
New Zealand: www.thegoodbook.co.nz

North America: 866 244 2165
UK & Europe: 0333 123 0880
Australia: (02) 6100 4211
New Zealand (+64) 3 343 1990

www.christianityexplored.org

Our partner site is a great place for those exploring the Christian faith, with a clear explanation of the good news, powerful testimonies and answers to difficult questions.

One life. What's it all about?